MW01181990

All Scriptures taken from the New American Standard Bible unless otherwise quoted. All other Scriptures taken from the English Standard Version.

Scripture taken from the NEW AMERICAN STANDARD BIBLE © 1960, 1962,1963,1968, 1971,1972,1973,1975,1977, 1995 by The Lockman Foundation. Used by permission.

Scripture quotations are from The Holy Bible, English Standard Version® (ESV©), copyright © 2001 by Crossway Bibles, a publishing ministry of Good News Publishers. Used by permission. All rights reserved.

As Christ – A Man and Marriage
Second Edition, 2015
ISBN: 978-1515211921

Christ Died For His Bride, So What's Your Problem?
First Edition, 2011
ISBN: 978-1-60383-384-4

As Christ

A Men and Marriage

Jeremy B. Strang

Dedication

This book is dedicated to my Lord Jesus Christ, to Trish (my bride), and to my children. May I actually heed the words contained within! May every husband, and future husbands to be, have their eyes wide open, hear with ears unplugged, and respond with boldness as never before. May the Lord convict us of our sin and bring us to our knees, especially in regards to loving, serving, and ministering to our wives and families.

God's holiness is unfathomable, His grace is completely amazing, His mercy is relentless, His love is all encompassing, His justice is perfect, His forgiveness is undeserved, His presence is unexplainable – so who am I to say a word against His providence?

My Prayer

Taking into serious consideration the day and age that the sovereignty of God's hand has placed us, my prayer is for all men, including myself, to be grieved of our sins leading unto repentance.[1] That we would allow God to plow up the arid ground of our hearts with His Word and by His Spirit.

And how shall we move forward, fighting back the evils of this world in tearing down wickedness in high places? How shall we be about the right path of God honoring love and service to our wives in Christ? How shall we be the example we are called to be? So as was said to Zerubbabel, so is said to us, *"Not by might, nor by power, but by My Spirit says the Lord of hosts."*[2]

So let us move forward making the best use of our time.[3] May we set our sights [4] clearly on Christ, for *"He committed no sin, neither was deceit found in His mouth. When he was reviled, he did not threaten, but continued entrusting Himself to Him who judges justly."*[5] Let us be men who are *as Christ* to our wives, our children, and to everyone we meet along the way. *"Let marriage be held in honor among all, and let the marriage bed be undefiled, for God will judge the sexually immoral and adulterous."*[6]

---

[1] 2 Corinthians 7:10
[2] Zechariah 4:6
[3] Ephesians 5:15-16
[4] Hebrews 12:1-4
[5] 1 Peter 2:22-23
[6] Hebrews 13:4

Forward
Caleb Gordon[7]

"Husbands, love your wives, as Christ loved the church and gave himself up for her."[8]

Guys-
Are most of us really doing this? I mean, are we really? Are we laying our lives out on the line for our wives, expecting nothing in return? So many men do things to "HELP" their ladies, but it is with an underlying motive? – and you all know what kind of motive I'm talking about. This is foolish! I will be honest. I have been guilty of this in the past. But it's not something real men should do, especially if you're claiming to be a Christ follower. How is this to be lived out? Just the way God called it to be. Love your wife THE WAY JESUS LOVES YOU – even when you're in a "mood." God does not get short with you when you're complaining and grumpy...what does he do? He pursues you more, letting you know that He loves you and wants a real relationship with you. As a result of this, what happens? He draws you in closer.

---

[7] Husband, Father, Blogger, Communicator – www.calebgordon.com
[8] Ephesians 5:25

"Husbands, love your wives, and do not be harsh with them."[9]

Don't be harsh with the wife that you chose to love. Instead continue to love her, and lay yourself out for her. I truly do believe that if men would stand up and love their wives with a sacrificial kind of love, that women would have no issue doing the *"submitting"* part of Ephesians 5. They would love to be connected to a man who is leading them spiritually, loving them sacrificially, and emptying themselves on her behalf. I know that when I make an effort to do this with my wife she is beaming with joy and contentment.

What Jeremy is doing through this book is giving us a model of what it looks like to love our wives like Christ loves us. As you turn the pages of this book I firmly believe you'll be challenged, encouraged, and enlightened. Jeremy is one who uses God's word to speak straight to your heart. He has a desire to see men come under the direction of God's Holy Spirit in every aspect of their marriage. I know that you are going to enjoy this journey you are about to travel while reading through this book. Read carefully and allow the Holy Spirit to lead you.

MAN UP!

---

[9] Colossians 3:19

2nd Forward
Warren Judge[10]
(1st edition)

*"Husbands, love your wives, as Christ loved the church
and gave Himself up for her, that he might sanctify her,
having cleansed her by the washing of water with the
word, so that he might present the church to Himself in
splendor, without spot or wrinkle or any such thing, that
she might be holy and without blemish. In the same way
husbands should love their wives as their own bodies. He
who loves his wife loves himself".[11]*

Are these Scriptures still for today or have we become so
complacent in this world that we refuse to obey the truth
of God's Word? I believe they still ring aloud today as
when Paul wrote them from prison almost two thousand
years ago.

How many times have we read or heard this passage but
yet as men we always go back to the verse that reads,
wives submit yourself to your husbands, as to the Lord?

Why are we so quick to think that our wives must submit
first just so we can escape our responsibility to them? In
reality as men we have the greater challenge ahead of us.

---

[10] Close friend and brother in Christ
[11] Ephesians 5:25-28 ESV

In all due respect gentlemen, we are the ones who must submit first and this to the Lord. We have a command to love them from Christ, not only as our brides, but as sisters in the Lord. As husbands we have a responsibility to present our wives without spot or blemish and to be holy to the Lord.

I know sometimes as men this can be hard since we usually look to our own needs first before our spouses. I know in my own life this has been a challenge and I need greater discipline and prayer in Christ to continue my daily responsibilities. If we are going to serve the Lord, we need to serve and love our wives first before ourselves, just as Christ showed in serving His bride, the church.

In his new book, *'Christ Died For His Bride, So What's Your Problem?'*, Jeremy Strang opens a door using God's Word and sheds light on our past misfortunes of self-serving lifestyles, commanded obedience, and the lustful and selfish desires we have demanded from our wives. With Scripture and personal testimonies, Jeremy shows we can find a path from the Word of God to repent and seek forgiveness from Christ and our wives. Jeremy pulls no punches here. He comes through with great conviction on our responsibility to honor and love our wives for the glory of Jesus Christ. He leaves you with the challenge that one of our greatest testimonies we can leave is in our service to Christ through the loving of our wives. May we always serve Christ in loving and honoring our wives.

Intro

It is through Jesus Christ that we may know *the mystery of His will*.[12] His will was set forth in Christ as a plan *to unite all things in Him.*[13] His will has been clearly revealed to His children and executed through the loving of their wives and the loving of the brethren. Whoever does not love abides in death. *Everyone who hates his brother is a murderer; and you know that no murderer has eternal life abiding in Him.*[14] To love as God loves is a continuous desire of every true Christian.

Verbally saying that you love your wife means absolutely nothing if you yourself are not consumed by the true love[15] that Christ Himself supplies. All forms of loving your wife without the power of God's love, *as Christ loved the church,*[16] will fail. Often our love is centered on our own humanistic appetites, and when backed by a profession of faith,[17] we stand to be held accountable on

---

[12] Ephesians 1:9
[13] Ephesians 1:9b-10 ESV – (capitalizations of Him, He, His are mine showing emphasis on God are throughout this book)
[14] 1 John 3:15
[15] agape
[16] Ephesians 5:25
[17] Matthew 7:21-23

judgment day. If our Christian claim is not valid, our very best works for our wives will be burned as dross from silver leaving us as dead waste awaiting eternal damnation.

If indeed we do not love our wives by the power of God's love, we give way to the possibility that we are unregenerate.[18] Can this be said of us? If yes, we need to clearly see that we are destined for eternal torment while temporarily suspended over hell's grips.[19] If we profess Christ in our life, we should be diligent and careful to love our wives as Christ has displayed for us.[20] As Christ died for His bride He showed no anger, no rebellion, no retaliation, but displayed complete denial of self;[21] all the while, it was His forthcoming bride[22] who was putting Him to death. He stood in our law place[23] even though we deserved to be condemned forever.

How can we ever run to the risen Savior and say, *"I deserve a right to get even because of how my wife is treating me?"* To love our wives as Christ loves the church, means we must understand His sacrifice, His gospel, His commands, and His price of redemption; it also means we must admit our guilt, expose our failures, examine our present spiritual condition, repent of our sinful ways, and seek God as never before.

A man who does not deny himself and sacrifice all worldly pleasures for his wife is not devoted to God as he

---

[18] Never having been saved; no conversion

[19] Thought owed to Jonathan Edwards – *Sinners in the Hands of an Angry God*

[20] and in those of us who have truly been born again

[21] 1 Peter 2:21-25

[22] Meaning it was rebellious, sinful and depraved man prior to salvation

[23] Romans 5:6-8; 2 Corinthians 5:21

may think.[24] Marriage exists and *refers to Christ and the church;* in other words, Christ and His bride.[25] Jesus refers to Himself as the bridegroom[26] and if we are truly a part of His Church, then we must act as He expects – a bride in preparation for her wedding day.

Men, let's prove the authenticity of our faith through sacrificial love, denial of our selfish desires, and a God honoring commitment to uphold the covenant relationship we have made with our wives.[27] May we seek to be

---

[24] 1 John 4:20

[25] Ephesians 5:32

[26] Matthew 9:15

[27] The marriage covenant was established by God early in human existence. The idea of covenant was God's plan and promise for the redemption of Israel. Marriage is displayed by God throughout the Old Testament in His love for Israel. In the New Testament, Christ displays His love for the church as a bridegroom who loves His bride, especially when she did not deserve to be loved. Christ's display of love for His Church is the ultimate example of how a husband's love for his wife ought to be. The unity Christ has with His body and oneness with His Church (John 17:20-23) is the oneness and unity of a husband with his wife. *"For this reason a man shall leave his father and mother and shall be joined to his wife and the two shall become one flesh."* (Ephesians 5:31; Genesis 2:24; Matthew 19:5) Please note that the purpose of this writing is not to debate theology. I also don't wish to debate whether the KJV is correct as it refers to the Church in Ephesians 5 as *"it"*. The ESV, NASB, and NKJ all agree that the proper translation that Paul refers to the Church in Ephesians 5 is *"her"*. Usage of the feminine word *her* does not refer to men as women nor does it give approval for homosexual relationships. Ephesians 5 does not refer to any one individual as the bride of Christ; rather this refers to the Church as a corporate whole. To this end, whenever I refer to Christ's bride, I am referring to the Church. The purpose of this writing is to call husbands to deny themselves and truly love their wives. *Bride of Christ* – those who are

sanctified[28] all of our days, and may we carry this working onto fulfilling God's plan for marriage in the privacy of our homes and in light of a godless world.

Additional Note:

Having said these things, I want to be completely up front regarding the timing of this edition and a new chapter that I was intending to add at the end. If there has ever been a chapter I find exceedingly difficult to write, without a doubt, it is the one regarding the topic of knowing the good I ought to do and not doing it as it relates to my marriage. I find that it is absolutely necessary for me, at this time, to let God's Word do a more thorough cleansing in me before I put it to publish; let me try to express my concerns.

---

regenerated by the Holy Spirit and given a new heart; the corporate whole of regenerated believers who are in a process of sanctification and leading unto righteous deeds and dressed in fine linen. The bride of the Lamb is the New Jerusalem and *nothing unclean will ever enter it, nor anyone who does what is detestable or false, but only those who are written in the Lamb's book of life* [Revelation 21:27]. Whether the New Jerusalem is a real physical place or whether it is just a representation of a spiritual reality [as some do believe] in God's kingdom is not the main concern. The author's concern regarding this is for all to take note that the New Jerusalem will be filled with the Glory of God and lit by the living Savior, and only those who are in the *book of life* having been regenerated by Christ, the Bridegroom Himself, will be present.

[28] The process by which we are continually growing in holiness, purity, and righteousness through the person of Christ Jesus. It is to be in a continual process of being washed by the word of God and transformed in the inner man.

It should be no surprise that the timing of the Devil and all his schemes would shoot arrows upon all aspects of my soul, my flesh, and my good intentions. And yet, to be merely cognitive of this war does not give me any excuse to be lax in repentance of my sins and to actually *"do the good I know I ought."*[29] For if I do not act accordingly, it would be far better to turn my pen from the paper into a dagger for the killing of my flesh,[30] a sword for the slicing of the ungodly intentions of my heart. It would be better for me to cut off my hand than to sin.[31] Indeed the words of Jeremiah ring true:

"Cursed is the man who trusts in man and makes flesh his strength, whose heart turns away from the Lord."[32]

and…

"The heart is deceitful above all things, and desperately sick; who can understand it?"[33]

I find that I must be about the renewing of my mind,[34] about the putting to death of my sin,[35] and the right motivations, convictions and power of the Spirit.[36] For without the conviction of the Spirit of God, the right motivation to honor God, and having a rooting, the very

---

[29] James 4:17
[30] For those who do not understand this type of speech, please read and study the context of Romans 8:13.
[31] Matthew 5:30, 18:8
[32] Jeremiah 17:5
[33] Jeremiah 17:9
[34] Romans 12:1-2
[35] Romans 8:13
[36] Zechariah 4:6

centering upon Christ alone, I am unable to completely fulfill the *good* unto my wife and my family.

Oh what a hopeless state I would remain if I were without the true working grace of God! Oh wretched man I am is right![37]

May the Lord be pleased to grant me, once again, repentance deep in my soul. I need a complete renewal by Christ, so that I may become more of a *"living sacrifice"*[38] for the spiritual worship and obedience to my Lord – this I pray for the eternal building of my wife and family and to the eternal end of God's glory. And truly this I will do if I willfully choose to carry my cross and deny myself.[39]

"For the kingdom of God does not consist of talk, but of power."[40]

---

[37] Romans 7:24
[38] Romans 12:1
[39] Luke 9:23
[40] 1 Corinthians 4:20

"This is a profound mystery—but I am talking about Christ and the church (Ephesians 5:32). The Apostle Paul speaks in a way here that 'pulls the blinders off,' showing the true intention of the marriage covenant, one standing for an eternal purpose and symbol. The Church, and God's relationship with this Bride, is the greater reality of what earthly marriage should point to. Our faithfulness to our wife in this earthly marriage speaks of the mystery of God's love for His people, the Church. Marriage is temporary in this life, and yet at the same time, the Church's covenant with God is eternal. Happy is the man and woman who looks beyond themselves to eternity and what this life all points towards."

- Greg Gordon, *founder SermonIndex.net*

You can tell how a man loves God, by the way he treats his family.

- Dan Frost, *pastor and friend*

As Christ ~ A Man and Marriage

From the Ladies

"In response to your question, 'What does it mean to me that my husband follows Christ first in our marriage,' I would have to admit that it can be terrifying... to my flesh. When I see my husband run headlong after Christ, I know that my biblical response as a wife should be that of great joy, but I often must battle the enemy and my own flesh. I catch myself wondering, 'What if he turns our life upside down?' And yet, in these times, I sense the Spirit answering, 'What if that's what Jesus wants?' I am reminded that Billy and I serve the same Jesus and He certainly doesn't call us to a cushy Christianity. So, while my flesh may tremble at my husband seeking Christ above all else, it is my spirit that finds joy."

~ Elizabeth

From the Ladies is based off the question: *What does it mean to you that your husband follows Christ first and foremost in his life?* All of the ladies are professing believers and the status of their husband's salvation was of insignificance.

Walk With God

Enoch walked with God[41]

*T*he *greatest need in the world is a godly man. The greatest need of my wife is a godly man. The greatest need of my children is a godly man.*[42] The foundational problem with many marriages today begins here – we simply do not want God. I ask professing believers all the time what it means to be a Christian and have a *relationship* with God; most cannot give me an answer that is biblically backed by Scripture. They tell me what they do, where they go, and what they believe, but rarely do I hear that they know God, walk with Him, desire Him, understand His will,[43] and God forbid, fall under any conviction in regards to their sin. Often people tell me that God wants them to do something, go somewhere, read this, and listen to that, but then they never do it. At the same time, they are completely mesmerized by every sort of gadget, movie, song, book, and even so called *Christian* things that are not biblical at all. So was it God, or their lying emotions? The answer is all too obvious.

---

[41] Genesis 5:24
[42] Paul Washer, *The Christian Husband*-www.sermonaudio.com
[43] Jeremiah 9:23-24

What does it really mean to walk with God? Look at Enoch, no Bibles, no fellowship groups, no church buildings, no books describing God, nothing at all, but God Himself – and He was more than enough! We have everything he did not have and yet most professing believers in the Western world have little to no biblical knowledge of the God who supposedly saved them. These same professing believers have never experienced the reality of salvation. Their knowledge and understanding of God's will in their life, including knowing what He hates and what He commands, seems to be more related to myth and personal belief rather than Scriptural truth. Is it any wonder that the professing church in the West looks just like the world in all its fallen state? Is it any wonder that marriage is so undervalued and our wives are so mistreated? Is it any wonder that our young generation does not value marriage? Is it any wonder that homosexuality is out of control? No. Why would these things be a shock when we do not cherish the person of Christ, seek holiness,[44] and grow in the understanding of what it means to walk with God?

> *"To walk with God is to set God always before us, and to act as those that are always under His eye. It is to live a life of communion with God both in ordinances and providences. It is to make God's word our rule and His glory our end in all our actions. It is to make it our constant care and endeavour in everything to please God, and nothing to offend Him. It is to comply with His will, to concur with His designs, and to be workers*

---

[44] Hebrews 12:14

together with Him. It is to be followers of Him as dear children."[45]

It is to be known by God[46] and walk in His very presence. Look at Jacob; he wrestled with God until a blessing was poured out. He did not give up even though he paid a price.[47]

If we are serious about becoming the husbands for our wives that God has required of us, we must first recognize and admit that we are married more to the world than we are to our own wives. We are adulterers and fornicators who display all forms of sexual immorality, and thereby we deserve death.[48] We need to quit being yoked with the unbelieving and darkened world.[49] We must come to a very sobering realization that our wives are God's daughters first and our wives second. Mistreating God's daughters is a very serious offense and one punishable by eternal death. A man's failure is that he does not recognize the reality of Who ultimately and eternally loves his wife more than he ever could – her Father in heaven; and without truly abiding with the Father, how could we recognize His daughter? Without an authenticity of knowing God, how can you know her elder brother?[50]

So what does it mean to carry out a divorce with the world? To divorce the world is to identify, in your own life, all the sinful desires, thoughts, and ways, and then to be

---

[45] Matthew Henry, Matthew Henry's Commentary, Vol. 1, pg. 40, copyright 1991 by Hendrickson Publishers, Inc., eighth printing-April 2006
[46] Matthew 7:23; 1 Corinthians 8:2-4
[47] Genesis 32:22-32
[48] 1 Corinthians 6:9-10
[49] 2 Corinthians 6:14
[50] Jesus Christ – *first born among many brethren* – Romans 8:29

about the killing[51] of these besetting sins. The question then must be asked, how do I kill these things? The answer comes by the washing of the water through the Word of God[52] and by devoted, intimate, real, and close communion with God Himself. It is to be in authentic prayer and by His Spirit. Let me give you some examples.

If my flesh does not want to be devoted to prayer, then I set devoted time to prayer and begin a violent warring against myself to do so. If while I am in prayer I keep wondering in thought and desire to leave devoted prayer, then I take *violence*[53] against myself and drop back down resetting my sights to God's presence once again. When my flesh desires to eat for no real reason, then I violently deny myself the things that carry me into sinful gluttony by putting the food back on the shelf. When I see something that visually stimulates me, I run like a wild-man away[54] from the temptation as if it were going to crush me and drag me to hell. When ministry or mere Bible reading surpasses my prayer life and communion with God, I take violence against my flesh by admitting that I have been feeding my own vain glory[55] and self-righteousness against others. I turn in repentance and set my sights to the fellowship of God and then tarry with God in prayer. This is just a part of what it means to kill the flesh, to begin a divorce with the world, and to be resolved in seeking the presence of God Himself. This is what Jesus means when He says *if your hand causes you*

---

[51] Romans 8:13

[52] Ephesians 5:26; Romans 12:2

[53] Not physically, but a warring in the Spirit to root out my flesh-driven desires to leave

[54] *flee*, 1 Corinthians 6:18

[55] Thought owed to Paul Washer; [*vain glory* – excessive pride in ones own performance, attainments, importance, etc. The vaunting of oneself – Terry Light]

to sin cut it off.[56] Taking action against the sin in your life through deeply looking unto the true grace of Christ[57] is the only way of divorcing the world.

To commune with God begins in relentless prayer and a deep desire to know God's glory. Look at the perseverance of the widow in Luke 18:1-8. She consistently pursued the judge until he gave in. Is this not how we ought to seek God in prayer? Take the desire of Moses to know God's glory, he, by faith, truly desired to know God in a greater way.[58] He desired to know Him intimately and know His ways. Is this not a desire to know the very person of God Himself?

Now you may be saying that I am some legalist, and to you I reply: if it is a killing of the flesh, a killing of sinful desires, and killing of that which keeps us from having an authentic and intimate relationship with God, then it is not legalism. Maybe your own flesh is crying out legalism because you really are not concerned with personal holiness, intimacy with God, and a true abiding with the Holy Spirit? It may well be that it is you yourself that has fallen into a legalism of flesh whereby you desire to feed your intellect, your emotions, your sickly appetites, and your self-righteous mental domination over someone else. Do you need to wake up to your present spiritual state and leave others alone? Have you entered the narrow gate and are you walking on the narrow path?[59] Allow God to set your paths straight. The best interest for your wife is for you to kill your selfishness, repent, and be sanctified. Maybe then the Lord will use you as a vessel of honor;

---

[56] Matthew 5:30-31
[57] See authors book, *The Foothills of True Grace*
[58] Exodus 33:12-23
[59] Matthew 7:13-14

honor in your life, honor in your ministry, and honor in your marriage.

Walking with God and a divorcing of this world will cost you. Are you willing to pay the price? We need to be men who are like Shadrach, Meshach and Abednego. We need to refuse to fall down and worship the golden image.[60] We need to have a very real salvation which leads to a very real dedication to be able to stand firm and say,

> *"O Nebuchadnezzar, we do not need to give you an answer concerning this matter. If it be so, our God whom we serve is able to deliver us from the furnace of blazing fire; and He will deliver us out of your hand, O king. But even if He does not, let it be known to you, O king, that we are not going to serve your gods or worship the golden image that you have set up.*"[61]

Our refusal to stand against the world and its system is false idol worship. We constantly serve a master, either the Father in heaven or the father of lies. If we profess Christ and yet walk in opposition to our claim, we present *defiled food upon* God's altar. Read the book of Malachi in light of how you have walked with the Father and how you have treated His daughter. The best thing we can do is *close the doors* on everything that we hold dear to us that is not of God. Everything that takes our thoughts away from His glory must be killed. We should slam shut the doors of our self-centered desires that takes time and energy away from God's daughters. *'A son honors his father, and a servant his master. Then if I am a father, where is My honor? And if I am a master, where is My*

---

[60] Daniel 3:8-12
[61] Daniel 3:16-18

respect?' says the LORD of hosts to you, O priests who despise My name.[62] Can you imagine your wife saying this to you? It would be bad enough for your wife to declare such a thing, but can you imagine how much worse this would be coming from the mouth of God? I dare say many of you reading, may now possibly deserve to be told this either, because you have not been sanctified and transformed by the renewal of your mind,[63] or you have yet to experience God's grace in authentic salvation. Is your walk with God validated by His Word and a testimony of His Spirit,[64] or your belief?

The declaration of how you serve your God and how you treat your wife is not in word, but it is in power, by the Spirit, and in love. If the kingdom of God exists in power,[65] how much more should our devotions to Christ and our love for our wives be displayed through a reckless abandon of our selfish ways and a sacrificial dying for our bride? How are we to demonstrate our love – is it not in humility, mercy, grace, and self-denial of Christ? Rise up O man of God, or are you a hypocritical unregenerate who smiles while walking dead into a church building on Sunday mornings?

This is about the power of God flowing through a man, and his ministry of the Word unto His wife.[66]

Reality starts with an acknowledgement that many of us do not have a walk with God at all. We must admit that we

---

[62] Malachi 1:6
[63] Romans 12:2
[64] Romans 8:16-17
[65] 1 Corinthians 4:20
[66] Paul Washer, Message: *The Christian Husband*

have mistreated many of God's daughters and that we have mocked the *marriage bed* in general.[67]

Prayer:

God help us to repent, to walk with You in truth, to authentically desire Your Son, and to live a sacrificial life of love for our wives. May we close the doors on all of our false worship, stand firm while facing the fire, and divorce our yoke of narcissism.[68] Amen.

Therefore as you have received Christ Jesus the Lord, so walk in Him, having been firmly rooted and now being built up in Him and established in your faith, just as you were instructed, and overflowing with gratitude. See to it that no one takes you captive through philosophy and empty deception, according to the tradition of men, according to the elementary principles of the world, rather than according to Christ.[69]

---

[67] Hebrews 13:4
[68] Excessive consumption with self
[69] Colossians 2:6-8

From the Ladies

"What it means to me that my husband is following Christ is by the evidence of the fruit I'm seeing. He is taking the initiative to read the Word of God. He is also attending a local body and turning his ear to hear the Spirit of the Lord speak to him through the Holy Spirit residing within him. I am also seeing that he is putting others before himself like Christ gave Himself up for the Church. That is the fruit I am witnessing in my husband."

~ Christine

Love Never Fails

Love never fails.[70]

*L*ove never fails, unless of course we live by only our human concept of love, an emotionally based self-pleasing love. Without a desire for sanctification through the reality of knowing God firsthand, then our love falls far short of God's perfect love, for He Himself is love.[71] Without sanctification, there is no decisive evidence that we are walking with the Lord. For if we ourselves, without the love of God, remain empty, we thereby leave our wives in dry places.[72] If we do not have the true love of God in us, then how far will our human love get us past the gates of the kingdom of heaven? Not even one inch!

If human love does not have the ability to get us in the kingdom's doors, then why should we allow such a limited and powerless type of love to entertain our minds

---

[70] 1 Corinthians 13:8
[71] 1 John 4:8; read all of 1 John
[72] Not saying at all that our wives do not have the obligation to seek God for themselves as individuals. But rather, a reminder, this book was written for men and not women.

and drive our marriages?[73] I submit to you two possible answers.

First, as mentioned before, we are married to the world more than our wives. Our marriage to the world is willfully engaged in our passivity and our deceptive self-serving emotions. Our emotions often leave us pride-filled, self-centered, and completely reliant upon receiving more and more attention in order to feed the yoke of bondage to the flesh and our old sinful nature. This condition of the heart will always limit any type of self-promoted love, thus our love fails.

The second reason that I believe we love our wives with only a mere human love is that we are ignorant of what the Gospel of Jesus Christ and His finished work of grace really cost. This is no small problem and nothing to make little of. It is the foremost problem in failing marriages, and in a great many men who profess to be Christians. Let's take a glance at the model Christ has for marriage. I encourage an ongoing lifelong study in this area.

The model Christ has left for us in marriage has not been hidden. Understanding the Gospel of Jesus Christ and the picture of biblical marriage is unfathomable and truly a *mystery*,[74] and yet, one we must understand. If we remain ignorant to the truth, having only been spoon-fed a half-gospel, our abilities of dying for our bride and loving her like Christ is so much more difficult. If we remain ignorant of Christ's unfailing love, we'll be left with a *lottery type* of marriage; a marriage definitely not God

---

[73] I would suggest really studying 1 Corinthians 13:1-13; 8:1-3, not just reading/skimming it, but really studying these passages
[74] Ephesians 5:32

honoring or protected when temptation knocks at our door. So what is the model that Christ has left for us?

1. Christ demonstrated His love for His bride even when His bride did not love Him back.

God demonstrates His own love towards us, in that while we were yet sinners, Christ died for us. [75] This is completely astonishing and intellectually unfathomable. How is it that *He made Him who knew no sin to be sin on our behalf, so that we might become the righteousness of God in Him?*[76] Who could ever, even into eternity future, understand the full realm of God's grace? This is what's so unbelievable and foolish to most people – how did this Jesus become a payment for sin? His grace and His propitiation simply are an unthinkable kind of love.[77]

We must seek to understand that God loves us so much that He gave us, unto the death, His only Son – what an incomprehensible love.[78] We spend so little time, so little energy, so little thought, and so little study of the Gospel that we are completely ignorant of the ramifications of not doing so in regards to marriages. Add to this so little of a walk with God, and we are left with absolutely nothing to give to our marriages. Our wives receive nothing because we have nothing; the conclusion in her eyes therefore must be that God is nothing. This is our position with God, again in her eyes, if our life is not stamped with the presence of God Himself and a willing obedience to do what He desires. Do we dare be honest? So where do we go from here?

---

[75] Romans 5:8
[76] 2 Corinthians 5:21
[77] See author's book, *"The Foothills of True Grace."*
[78] John 3:16

First, we ought not to just merely read verses like 1 Corinthians 5:21 and move onto other things. We need to diligently seek to understand the glory of God and the sufferings of Christ that paid for our wretched souls. We also need to recognize that we are completely depraved and an abomination unto God if we have not been *cleansed of our filthiness*, given a *new heart*, given His *Spirit*,[79] and had His *laws written* on our new heart.[80] Without this being a reality, we can give our wives nothing of any eternal value. Our only guarantee will be a more severe punishment because we were *neither hot nor cold*,[81] but we chose to ride the fence, rejecting God's best for our marriage, and hurt His dear daughter in the process. Husbands, we will pay dearly if we are ignorant of His true Gospel and yet profess to be something that we are not.[82] We would be much better off to stop our ministry pursuits, lay down our church positions, and admit our need for repentance.

Moving forward in our marriages requires that we *examine ourselves*,[83] repent if needed, and walk with God. We must no longer take Scripture as secondary to our feelings and beliefs. If Jesus says that He is *the*[84] *way, the truth, and the life*,[85] then it is true.[86] Why would we want

---

[79] Ezekiel 36:25-27

[80] Jeremiah 31:31; Hebrews 8:7-13

[81] Revelation 3:15-16

[82] I suggest a detailed study of Matthew 7. If these passages of Scripture do not scare you to the point of self examination and repentance of sin, then know that you may be the very one who will fulfill the prophecy of Matthew 7:21-23.

[83] 2 Corinthians 13:5

[84] Meaning the *only*

[85] John 14:6

[86] 2 Timothy 3:16; Proverbs 30:5-6

to walk with the world straight into hell? Would it not be far better for us to run to the Father now? Christ is the *only way* to the Father and the only way to love our wives.

But now apart from the Law the righteousness of God has been manifested, being witnessed by the Law and the Prophets, even the righteousness of God through faith in Jesus Christ for all those who believe; for there is no distinction; for all have sinned and fall short of the glory of God, being justified as a gift by His grace through the redemption which is in Christ Jesus; whom God displayed publicly as a propitiation in His blood through faith. This was to demonstrate His righteousness, because in the forbearance of God He passed over the sins previously committed; for the demonstration, I say, of His righteousness at the present time, so that He would be just and the justifier of the one who has faith in Jesus.[87]

For you have been called for this purpose, since Christ also suffered for you, leaving you an example for you to follow in His steps, who committed no sin, nor was any deceit found in His mouth; and while being reviled, He did not revile in return; while suffering, He uttered no threats, but kept entrusting Himself to Him who judges righteously; and He Himself bore our sins in His body on the cross, so that we might die to sin and live to righteousness; for by His wounds you were healed. For you were continually straying like sheep, but now you have returned to the Shepherd and Guardian of your souls.[88]

A serious study of these texts, and the entire Bible, is what a husband who is serious about his wife and about his marriage will do. We must seek God with a reckless

---

[87] Romans 3:21-26
[88] 1 Peter 2:21-25

abandon in regards to our own desires, our own thoughts and our own ways, so that our *mind will be renewed*[89] enabling us to rightly worship in *Spirit and truth*.[90] Then we will understand the need to love, lead, and care for God's daughters. Otherwise, our love fails.

2. Christ fore-walked the way of leading His bride.

And he said to all, 'If anyone would come after me, let him deny himself and take up his cross daily and follow me. Whoever would save his life will lose it, but whoever loses his life for my sake will save it. For what does it profit a man if he gains the whole world and loses or forfeits himself? For whoever is ashamed of me and of my words, of him will the Son of Man be ashamed.'[91]

If we do not walk, as a style of life, in a passionate pursuit to follow Jesus as He has declared, how can we biblically lead our wives in a way that is eternally secure and eternally lasting?

i. Deny yourself – *yet not my will, but Yours be done*.[92]

One of the greatest examples that Jesus Christ left for us is His willing desire to deny Himself all His rights. Can you say, *not my will, but Yours be done*, in the context of your walk with God and in regards to your marriage?

---

[89] Romans 12:1-2
[90] John 4:24
[91] Luke 9:23-26
[92] Luke 22:42

It is our job as men to be on our faces petitioning God for our sanctification and for the presence of God so that we become like His Son. It is important to our wives' spiritual condition that we walk with God. We must be *continually transformed by the renewal of* our minds.[93] The more our thinking is set right with the will of God, the more we will biblically love our wives through the supernatural power of Christ's love.

If we are growing in sanctification then we must deny ourselves. We are to be warriors against our own flesh at three, four, five in the morning, or whatever time whereby we seek God in prayer. We are to fight for our wives and our families on our knees and war against our flesh in such a way that draws us unto God; war begins on the floor. In our fight, we are to convene with God Himself and hear clearly His marching orders. On the surface this may seem hard and unproductive, but a sweet fellowship with the Father is born here.

"We will either concentrate in prayer or pray in concentration camps."[94]

We need to come to a point where our going to God is no longer about our feeble prayers and wants but transitions into a total resting in the effectual presence of God's glory. Denial of ourselves is to place every thought, every prayer, every cry, everything, second to the person of Christ Jesus and the fellowship with the Almighty. It is to deny ourselves everything that sets itself as a road block in front of our Lord.

---

[93] Romans 12:2
[94] Leonard Ravenhill

Guard your steps as you go to the house of God and draw near to listen rather than to offer the sacrifice of fools; for they do not know they are doing evil. Do not be hasty in word or impulsive in thought to bring up a matter in the presence of God. For God is in heaven and you are on the earth; therefore let your words be few. For the dream comes through much effort and the voice of a fool through many words.[95]

I am not at all suggesting that we always sit in some sort of false pious silence, yet there is a wonderful and powerful fellowship with God when nothing is spoken and we are out of the way. When, if ever, have you just rested in His presence? If never, or long ago, then know that denial of yourself and a running unto the throne needs to be swift and soon.

ii. Take up your cross daily – *Now those who belong to Christ Jesus have crucified the flesh with its passions and desires.*[96]

Take now your son, your only son, whom you love, Isaac, and go to the land of Moriah, and offer him there as a burnt offering on one of the mountains of which I will tell you.[97] What obedience on Abraham's part. Isaac was unaware of what was going to be placed upon the wood that he was carrying, but Abraham was well aware of the cross he was bearing. How burdensome it had to have been for Abraham during the three day journey to a mountain unknown. Abraham's faith and obedience to God was not easy, was not comfortable, and was not his plan; nonetheless he obediently carried out God's

---

[95] Ecclesiastes 5:1-3
[96] Galatians 5:24
[97] Genesis 22:2

commandment against all logic. He picked up his cross and followed his God with a total commitment. What a picture of the Lord Jesus Christ in this passage

We too, like Abraham, must pick up our cross. We must deny ourselves otherwise we will not pick up even the least of things for our God. Without the carrying of our cross we are not worthy to follow Christ.[98] You see the picking up of our cross leads to the crucifixion of our flesh, our passions, and our desires.[99] Our old nature is put to death through the denial of our selfish cravings and carried out in a steadfast resolve against temptation[100] for sin.[101] This process takes root in the new birth,[102] through the renewing of the mind,[103] and through an intimate prayer life with God. Our steadfastness, empowered by God's Spirit, results in the action of willfully doing[104] the opposite that our flesh desires to fulfill. To pick up our cross is to carry out a responsive action of obedience to Christ by performing what is seemingly impossible with a willingness to defy logical thought and fleshly emotions. It is to be hidden with Christ in God[105] having the convictions against sin by the Holy Spirit, thereby becoming a doer who actually does.[106]

Jesus Christ willingly endured the cross and despised the shame.[107] In Him there was no rebellion, no complaining,

---

[98] Matthew 10:38
[99] Galatians 5:24
[100] See James 1:13-16
[101] Colossians 3:5
[102] John 3
[103] Romans 12:2
[104] James 4:17 (or not doing depending upon the sin)
[105] Colossians 3:3
[106] James 1:22-24
[107] Hebrews 12:1-2

and no denying reality. Christ's only purpose was to do the will of His Father.[108] In this we find our problem. Unless we too are centered on the Father's will, we will not follow Christ. Any attempt to follow Christ by some mere intellectual ascent or means of bypassing repentance and the picking up of our cross, is a wretched blindness to our present spiritual state.

While it is true, that God *so loved the world that He gave His only Son*,[109] it is equally true that there is only *one way, one truth, and one life*[110] in which we must enter the kingdom of God. One who attempts to enter by any other door, is a thief and a robber.[111] God's love never gives us a justification to deny His commandments; God never contradicts Himself. Any husband who says he loves his wife and yet does not die to his prideful, self-lusting ways, does not love his wife *as Christ does the church*. Repentance and a turning unto Christ is the only way to escape the hell bound path to eternal death.

  iii. Follow Christ – *Do nothing from selfishness of empty conceit, but with humility of mind regard one another as more important than yourselves; do not merely look out for your own personal interests, but also for the interests of others*.[112]

Are you looking out for the *interests* of your wife or are you more concerned for your own selfish fulfillments? Are you *considering* your wife as more important than yourself? Are you serving her only to have your own needs met? Without the Spirit wrought about in our life

---

[108] Matthew 26:39; John 4:34, 5:30, 6:38 – for starters
[109] John 3:16
[110] John 14:6
[111] John 10:2
[112] Philippians 2:3-4

and a radically changed heart, doing as Christ did will be difficult, [113] joyless, completely burdensome, and short lived. It certainly will not lead unto eternal life nor demonstrate to our bride a picture of a godly man.

The ability to love our wives as we should is a product of following Christ and doing the will of the Father; even in these we are empowered by God as His love consumes us and motivates us into action. The reality of regeneration and a new heart full of God's love must be present. We are to deny self, die to the old flesh driven desires and to carry out the new birth in physical, mental, and spiritual truth. As mentioned earlier, Christ was consumed with the will of His Father. How much more should this be our desire and our driving force? The will of the Father is always perfect and always produces real spiritual fruit[114] as we walk through the sanctification process.

Is Christ your reality and chief concern? Is it your desire to please the Father? Is the fruit of your claim overflowing onto your wife or are you claiming something that is not a true reality in your life? What biblical assurances do you have backing your claim?

Beware of the false prophets, who come to you in sheep's clothing, but inwardly are ravenous wolves. You will know them by their fruits. Grapes are not gathered from thorn bushes nor figs from thistles, are they? So every good tree bears good fruit, but the bad tree bears bad fruit. A good tree cannot produce bad fruit, nor can a bad tree produce good fruit. Every tree that does not bear good fruit is cut

---

[113] if not next to impossible – even fleshly discipline can bring about some form of morality
[114] Galatians 5:22-23

down and thrown into the fire. So you will know them by their fruits. [115]

If I asked your wife what type of fruit you bear, what would she say? Would it be fruit of the Holy Spirit or fruit of the *prince of darkness*? Where do you pledge your thought life? Are sports a greater joy to you than spending time in the presence of your wife? Do you go to work to escape time with your family? Does Bible study choke out true fellowship with the One Who inspires and empowers the Word? Is your claim to Christianity more about what you do, where you go, and what you believe, or is it based on the person of Christ, fellowship with the Father, and obedience to the Spirit? Can you even see the difference?

Without a selfless abandoning of our conceited wants and desires we choose lesser things all while walking down the broad path. Without a true and intimate walk with the Savior we cannot love our wives as we are required. Without a denial of self, a crucifying of selfish longings, and a regenerated heart, we cannot be the husbands for our wives that the Bible commands and the culture so desperately needs, and our love fails.

3. **Christ sanctifies His bride.** *"When the LORD first spoke through Hosea, the LORD said to Hosea, 'Go, take a wife of harlotry and have children of harlotry, forsaking the LORD.'"* [116]

What a picture this leaves us. In a book about marriage you would not expect to see this passage, but give me room to explain because the picture here is very relevant for us today. After all, there may be men who are reading

---

[115] Matthew 7:15-20
[116] Hosea 1:2

this who are fornicating with other women outside of their marriage right now. And this passage is applicable for us all in some degree.

This is a very clear picture of Israel's rampant immorality, adultery, and denial of God. They were harlots in all aspects. This is also a very real picture of our Lord. He has come down from heaven being made a man, fulfilling the will of God, in order that He would make for Himself a bride. His bride did not deserve to be married, but deserved to die. At first, His bride started as a harlot but Jesus gave Himself totally up for a bride who deserved no love, no mercy, and no grace. Christ displayed His perfect love by completely denying Himself everything this world had to offer. Christ's bride did not deserve His grace, but oh how she greatly needed it.

Husbands, love your wives, just as Christ also loved the Church and gave Himself up for her, so that He might sanctify her, having cleansed her by the washing of water with the Word, that He might present to Himself the church in all the glory, having no spot or wrinkle or any such thing; but that she would be holy and blameless. So husbands ought to love their wives as their own bodies.[117]

Let me just ask you, are you in the process of sanctification? Notice how Christ sanctifies us, *by the washing of water with the Word.* If you yourself are not in the Word of God because of your great need to be sanctified, how could you even begin to understand your call of service to your wife? Your wife needs a husband who will sacrificially love her and cherish her. By sacrificial I mean, you are actually growing in personal holiness and growing in a hatred for the things of this

---

[117] Ephesians 5:25-28

world that pulls your attention off of Christ. A biblically sound husband must come to a point where the satisfaction of his emotions is laid bare and left to bleed upon the altar.

The only way that we can sanctify our wives is if we ourselves are submitted to the authority and discipline of the Almighty King of kings. If the Word of God is able to keep our way pure,[118] then why is the Word given such a small place in our lives? Do we actually believe that the Bible is the inspired Word of God or not?[119]

What is the source of your energy? From where do you seek your motivation and drive? Does your energy and excitement come from the gym, sports, hobbies, intellect, or the Word of God and His very presence? Stop thinking that you can somehow fool God, you cannot; stop playing games in your claim to Christianity; stop depriving your wife in your pride; stop deceiving yourself. There is no greater way that your wife needs you more than for you to be walking upright with the Savior. Crucify[120] your godless beliefs, your sin-loving desires, and your deceiving emotions, and seek the will of God[121] and His sanctification. Only then will your love be unfailing for your wife.

4. **Christ patiently waits.** *But do not let this one fact escape your notice, beloved, that with the Lord one day is like a thousand years, and a thousand years like one day. The Lord is not slow about His promise, as some*

---

[118] Psalm 119:9
[119] 2 Timothy 3:16-17
[120] Colossians 3:5
[121] Colossians 3:1-2

count slowness, but is patient toward you, not wishing for any to perish but for all to come to repentance.[122]

What patience the Lord demonstrates for us. He waits patiently towards us *not wishing for any* of us to perish. As He waits, we sin, and He still patiently waits. We wait until it is no longer comfortable to our flesh and then we retaliate. Sometimes our patience is only a few seconds. Look at what the Savior endured on our behalf and yet we who are to be His disciples constantly act out of our pride and faithlessness. The Lord tarries in patience while all mankind wages war against Him. His love is unfailing.

If you and I are truly in a process of transforming our lives into the person of Christ Jesus, then the fruits of the Spirit ought to be manifested. Two of these fruits of the Spirit are patience and self-control. These two areas have been a struggle in my life. These two fruits have brought me much conviction and discipline because in these two areas I often have fallen short; but praise God that He loves me so much that He disciplines me in my rebellion.[123] And praise God, because through Christ, I am continually making ground in these areas.

Inside my home is my greatest area of struggle. I struggle the most in my home because of two main reasons. I fail because I do not seek the sanctification of the Lord as I know I should. I fail because I have used my wife, and even my children, to my gain and their loss. What do I mean by this?

Whenever commonality roots itself through deceptive means, we become prey and blinded to the magnificent

---

[122] 2 Peter 3:8-9
[123] Hebrews 12:6

privilege God has given us in and through our wives. Whenever something becomes routine or common, we begin to lose sight of its value. Ever owned a new car? What happens five years later? It becomes a pile of junk. In actuality, it is our perception that has changed. The car was a dead pile of metal the moment it was bought. The same thing occurs in our marriages. Our perspective changes because our value towards our wife changes. Commonality is rooted in the deceptiveness of our pride, causing our focus to turn inward, our emotions scream selfishness, and our eyesight becomes darkened.

Listen to me clearly: you cannot think that you are justified in any retaliatory action against your wife. If she is disobedient to the Lord, then you cannot scream foul and strike back. Let the Lord bring her into conviction of sin. If you have been retaliating against your wife in any way, you must repent. Don't let the deceptiveness of commonality rob you.

One thing we must remember, repentance and faith are to be a style of our life. If these things are not evident, we have no assurance of our salvation. By the way, it is impossible to have true saving faith if you are not convicted of sin and led to repentance. Repentance and faith are not solo artists, they are a duet.

When the Son of Man comes, will He find faith on earth?[124]

Jesus is coming back and He will not be coming back with a lamb on His shoulders looking like some supermodel.[125] Commonality can destroy our patience, rob our self-

---

[124] Luke 18:8
[125] Thought owed to Voddie Baucham

control, and numb us to the reality of Christ's coming judgment. Christ is going to judge and make war.[126] How much more will He destroy all those who have mistreated His bride? How much more danger are you and I in if we mistreat God's daughters?

But the day of the Lord will come like a thief, and then the heavens will pass away with a roar, and the heavenly bodies will be burned up and dissolved, and the earth and the works that are done on it will be exposed.[127]

Be ready, for Christ is coming back. Be diligent to grow in patience and self-control. Fight hard against commonality. Let not even the sun go down on your anger.[128] Jesus is coming to rescue His bride and destroy those who have mistreated His body and profaned His name.[129] All rebels will be sent to hell and suffer forever. So, how are you treating your bride? Are you a rebel behind the doors of your private life?

Put on then, as God's chosen ones, holy and beloved, compassion, kindness, humility, meekness, and patience, bearing with one another and, if one has a complaint against another, forgiving each other; as the Lord has forgiven you, so you also must forgive. And above all these put on love, which binds everything together in perfect harmony. And let the peace of Christ rule in your hearts, to which indeed you were called in one body. And be thankful.[130]

---

[126] Revelation 19:11-16; also see Matthew 24:1-25:46 – for starters
[127] 2 Peter 3:10
[128] Ephesians 4:26
[129] Colossians 3:25
[130] Colossians 3:12-15 - ESV

For this is the will of God, your sanctification. For God has not called us for the purpose of impurity, but in sanctification. So, he who rejects this is not rejecting man but the God who gives His Holy Spirit to you.[131]

Pursue peace with all men, and the sanctification without which no one will see the Lord.[132]

Sanctify them in the truth; Your Word is truth. As you sent Me into the world, I have sent them into the world. For their sakes I sanctify Myself, that they themselves also may be sanctified in truth.[133]

May the Lord give us eyes to see and ears to hear and a mind to understand that *He has left us an example for us to follow in His steps* and to sacrificially die unto ourselves for our wives!

---

[131] 1 Thessalonians 4:3, 7-8
[132] Hebrews 12:14
[133] John 17:17-19

From the Ladies

"Seeing my husband grow in faith and give unto Him who sacrificed Himself for us, is the best gift he could ever give to me. Receiving guidance from my husband and knowing it comes from his heart, which holds the love of Jesus Christ, is reassuring. I know he puts Christ first and I can follow his lead without hesitation. This makes my heart content in our marriage. I love the passion he has for sharing his love for Christ with friends. It makes me feel proud to hold hands and share a life with a man who isn't afraid to proclaim his love for our Lord. What a joy and honor to be his wife."

~ Amanda

Even Your Marriage

And we know that for those who love God all things work together for good, for those who are called according to His purpose. For those whom He foreknew He also predestined to be conformed to the image of His Son, in order that He might be the firstborn among many brothers.[134]

This text is rich in so many ways. There is a promise for the truly regenerated believer; a clear declaration of faith; a way we are sanctified; a reason for our weaknesses and our wives weaknesses; a purpose for our marriages and so much more. There are four areas that I wish to give attention: to promise, to faith, to sanctification, and to our marriage and weaknesses.

1. In regards to promise –

The promise for those of us who have been born again is that *all things work together for* our good. One must be regenerated/born again/saved for this promise to be

---

[134] Romans 8:28-29 - ESV

fulfilled.[135] This means we must trust upon God's promise, even in the midst of tremendous trial. Have you been given a new heart? Has God written His laws upon your heart? Have you been regenerated? If you have not, then turn unto the Lord who gives us great help and promises for our eternal good, even in our marriages.

He saved us, not on the basis of deeds which we have done in righteousness, but according to His mercy, by the washing of regeneration and renewing by the Holy Spirit.[136]

We must be regenerated and found trusting in Christ for our every breath. We are not to lean on our own understanding,[137] but to depend upon the Holy Spirit in all things. We are to set our minds on the things above,[138] for the mind set on the flesh is death.[139]

Thus says the LORD, cursed is the man who trusts in mankind and makes flesh his strength, and whose heart turns away from the LORD. The heart is more deceitful than all else and is desperately sick; who can understand it?[140]

The promise of the *good* is only for those resting and trusting upon the risen Savior. Are you passionately trusting, loving, and obeying Jesus? Is He your all desiring commitment?

---

[135] See John 3, Ezekiel 36:22-32, 37:1-14; Jeremiah 31:31-34 – for starters
[136] Titus 3:5
[137] Proverbs 3:5
[138] Colossians 3:2
[139] Romans 8:7 – context 8:1-17
[140] Jeremiah 17:5, 9

In repentance and rest you shall be saved; in quietness and in trust shall be your strength.[141] Would your wife say that quietness and trust are your strengths? Is she witnessing the examples of repentance and rest in your life? Maybe you have not yet experienced the promise and understanding that conformity to Christ is indeed *good* and supreme in life. If not, no wonder that the, *"I do,"* you previously proclaimed to your wife is such a burden. No wonder that you are selfish and unloving; for without the reality of the new birth, you cannot see Christ's example to follow and promise to enjoy. If the Savior looks foolish and powerless in your eyes, then know that this promise is not yet yours.

2. **In regards to faith** –

For us to believe that *all things work together for good*, requires authentic faith that God knows what He is doing and He carries out the absolute best in our life. How can *all things* work for the *good* in our life? We cannot know the spiritual truths of Romans 8:28 unless we understand what *good* really means.

The *good* in verse 28 means *to be conformed to the image of His Son* in verse 29. This means that God will work all circumstances, people, struggles, pains, and even our mistakes to the *good to those who love Him, to those who are called according to His purposes.* This is especially true of our wives and our marriages as you will see. *Without faith it is impossible to please God*[142] and without faith there is no promise to your eternal *good*. Without an initial understanding of what eternally *good* means, tapping into the power of this passage in regards to your

---

[141] Isaiah 30:15
[142] Hebrews 11:6

marriage will prove fruitless and your application of sacrificial love for your wife will be joyless.

3. **In regards to sanctification** –

If God really *causes all things to work together* for our *good*, then we must recognize the reality that He is not calling us to our *best life now* and our continuous physical comfort. We must recognize that we will be wronged and that we ourselves will be wrong. I greatly appreciate what a pastor friend of mine recently said. He said, *"I would rather be the one who gets ripped off than be the one who rips others off."*[143] We must understand that God will use whatever means He deems necessary to transform our darkened thoughts and actions into the very image of His Son. God *causes* and continuously creates in us conformity to the person of Christ. He can do so exactly the way that He wants to, using whatever method He so desires.

Before redemption we were hell bent and completely depraved.[144] We were God haters and total lovers of self. If you don't believe these things, then you do not know your own sin or your true standing with the Father. If you don't believe that sin has been imputed to you; then you cannot believe, nor is it right for you to think, your sins to be imputed to Jesus Christ the Son of God.[145] To know you are saved means you have the awareness of what He saved you from – saved from yourself, saved from your

---

[143] Pastor Jack Olsen – Cornerstone Evangelical Free Church in Casper, WY
[144] Genesis 6:5
[145] Thought owed to Paul Washer; as talked about in the previous chapter

sin, and most importantly saved you from His just wrath.[146]

> *The Spirit Himself testifies with our spirit that we are children of God, and if children, heirs also, heirs of God and fellow heirs with Christ, **if indeed we suffer with Him** so that we may also be glorified with Him.*[147]

Before conversion we walked in the errors of our flesh. We built up and carried many patterns of sinfully governed thoughts, cravings, pursuits, and actions. It is a supernatural work God performs in causing *all things* to work for our eternal benefit. It is amazing grace which saves us and it is God's unimaginable sustaining power that continues to display His workings in our sanctification. As Leonard Ravenhill has said many times past, *"I believe it takes a greater act of God to take an unholy man out of the world, make him holy, put him back in an unholy world, and keep him holy."*

In causing *all things* to work together for our *good,* God displays His omniscience and His omnipotence. He reveals His controlled hand of sovereignty and great love He has for us. Because of His mercy, grace, and love, we are convicted of sin and brought to repentance; thus we are sanctified. His love disciplines us[148] and sets our ways straight. Without His kindness and disciplining love, we have no assurance of salvation and we are left with *the wrath of God* abiding upon us.[149] If this is indeed true of us, our wives are left void of a true man of God.

---

[146] Romans 5:8-9; I feel it necessary to mention this point again
[147] Romans 8:16-17
[148] Hebrews 12:4-11
[149] John 3:36

4. **In regards to our marriage and weaknesses** –

The weaknesses in both us and our wives are in us so that we will depend upon God, so we will realize our great need for the cross of Christ, and to provide us with a valuable example of Christ and His church. The weaknesses are meant to send us to the very throne of God for ever increasing depths in His presence and taking on His character. Christ displayed for us His true grace, unbelievable mercy, and unconditional love, such that we can never achieve in our own strength; this is all the reason more for the reality of regeneration and a fulfillment of dying to ourselves that Christ may increase.[150]

The reason for our divinely appointed weaknesses is so that we will learn unconditional love, sacrificial dying to self, and flesh defying humility. This comes through a true and raw comparison of ourselves in the light of the complete person of Christ. As a result of this comparison, we are to enter into a lifelong process of repentance. If indeed we approach the gatekeeper in this way, demonstration of love for our wives will become evident. It is through many weaknesses, failures, and pains that a sacrificial love for our wives will be produced – that is of course if we recognize our need for God and repent when convicted.

Unconditional has a hidden word, do you see it? Conditional, that is correct. If all your demands, dreams, expectations, rules, and conditions have been met through a perfect wife, then how do you display unconditional love? You cannot since all your requirements have been met.[151]

---

[150] John 3:30
[151] Thought owed to Paul Washer

When was the last time you praised God while in a trial?[152] When was the last time you asked God to continue burning out the dross in your life through a trial that was pressing you down? [153] When was the last time you thanked God that your wife has divinely orchestrated weaknesses that sometimes drive you crazy? If you are like me, you do not praise God as you should. Keep in mind, knowing the good that we ought to do and not doing is sin[154] and does not win any personal battles. Waging war with our flesh, in the fullness of Christ, is the only way we can positively answer such seemingly impossible questions.

If we desire to have a marriage that glorifies God, then we must do the things that we think are seemingly impossible. If we claim to be a Christian,[155] then we must do as the Bible commands otherwise we are not what we claim. If we claim to love our wives yet we never demonstrate the same sacrificial love that Christ displayed, then we do not love as we may think. We may see many failures and many problems in our wives, but I assure you God Himself sees every vile thought of ours. May we lay down our pride and seek Christ hard.

---

[152] James 1:2-4
[153] Thought owed to George Whitefield
[154] James 4:17
[155] Which by the way, the first Christians did not name themselves – Acts 11:26

From the Ladies

"First and foremost, I want to express the idea that if I did not have the Lord as my Savior and Comforter, I don't know if I would still be married to my husband. Now that he is saved, I believe we are on the same page in life as for making decisions together, praying about situations and raising our children in a godly way. Our relationship is amazing now that Jesus is the center of both of our lives and the blessings are abundant. The respect we have for one another is a whole new experience and I am excited to see what God has in store for us."

~ Cindy

'Til Death Do Us Part?

Brother Billy Witt – guest author

Is she really the one I'm supposed to be with?

Out of all the billions of women in the world, isn't there another that would make me happier?

Can't I follow the example of many in church leadership and find another wife more suited to me?

I'm certain some of you reading this book have probably asked similar questions. I know I certainly have. In frustrating moments I have allowed myself to be carried by my flesh and emotions, crying out to Christ asking such questions. I'd imagine Adam posed a few questions to God about his mate as well. We know for certain he said, *"the woman whom You gave to be with me, she gave me from the tree, and I ate."*[156] Based on this, I think it's safe to assume that He had discussions with God about the spouse he had been given! Perhaps he found himself

---

[156] Genesis 3:12

perplexed at times concerning her, not really understanding God's full plan of two becoming one.[157]

When asking such questions, I think the bigger question is: what will we do with our spouses? Shall we follow the example of many in the modern church? Shall we follow the advice of the world? Or shall we diligently follow the inward conviction and direction of the Holy Spirit and God's Word concerning them? What shall we do?

If we listen to the official advice (that which is written in books and preached in sermons) of most in the modern church, we will see that they advise that marriage is sacred and God intended it to be a lifelong commitment. And yet, if we watch how many, including those in leadership, actually live their lives, we will see something quite different. Many leaders in the modern church reveal, through the examples they live, that they themselves don't actually buy into the sanctity of marriage. Sadly many of these leaders are found committing adultery, divorcing their wives, and remarrying new ones. Should we follow suit?

The advice we find from the world differs from the official stance of the church, but at least those of the world practice what they preach! After reading secular books, hearing about what airs on television, and listening to our culture's music, we find that happiness is paramount, and our marital commitments should only be honored if they are satisfying. When such commitments are lacking the possibility of true happiness, the world suggests we should find that happiness by any means necessary. But does God want us to place such a high priority on our own happiness?

---

[157] Mark 10:8

My Personal Experience

"Put on the full armor of God, so that you will be able to stand firm against the schemes of the devil."[158]
"For our struggle is not against flesh and blood, but against the rulers, against the powers, against the world forces of this darkness, against the spiritual forces of wickedness in the heavenly places."[159]

As I begin, I want to stress that I am blessed with a great wife, especially since she met Christ and the Holy Spirit came to live within her. I'm certain that though we are not perfect, she is closer to reaching the goal through our Lord than I am. Now concerning my personal experience, around November of last year, I received a phone call from Brother Jeremy after we had recently visited with him and his wonderful family. During this conversation, he exhorted me to seek the Lord in prayer and to prepare for a spiritual attack as he sensed our enemy desired to sift me as he had Peter.[160] Shortly after this phone call and after I had finished publishing *Heavy Fog,* I noticed I was being plagued with thoughts about the past. These thoughts concerned things that I had forgiven my wife of over 13 years ago. Try as I might, I couldn't get the thoughts out of my mind. I studied Scripture, claimed my Lord's blood, commanded spirits to leave in His name, cried out to our Lord in prayer, and sought much counsel from my brethren, and especially brothers Patrick, Randy, Devin, Edgar and even my wife. I have never faced such a battle since being transformed by Jesus over 13 years ago.

---

[158] Ephesians 6:11
[159] Ephesians 6:12
[160] Luke 22:31

I read book after book concerning the issues I faced. Why now, after many years, was I suddenly being besieged by them? Most of the books offered terrible advice, though a few were a bit helpful. None offered a solution on how to stop what I was going through in a way that would be biblically pleasing to my Lord. Most of the books suggested moving on, divorce, adultery, or finding someone else. I was also plagued with thoughts concerning many of the professing church leaders, who after committing adultery, divorcing their wives, or marrying new ones, were still able to continue their ministry. Temptation to use grace as a license to sin, to follow the world, and to follow the poor advice of church leadership was ever present. Due to the stress, I lost around 40 pounds within the first three months. Losing the weight brought a host of admirers my way and this didn't ease the trial I was going through, instead made it all the more difficult to bear. I could feel demonic forces,[161] and my flesh trying to push me to grieve the Holy Spirit.[162] What would I do: follow men or God's Word?

I fasted, prayed, studied and kept seeking my brethren's help, encouragement, and prayers on the matter as I tried to understand it all. I knew I had genuinely forgiven her of these matters long ago. One day while driving home, and again crying out to the Lord with tears for understanding, the Spirit spoke clearly to me from within. He said plainly to me, "*Love her like Christ loved[163] the church.*"[164] It was this, in addition to God's Word reminding me, that "*God*

---

[161] Ephesians 6:12
[162] Ephesians 4:30
[163] This kind of love is a completely sacrificial one, it is divine in origin, and is to be given without any conditions being met and not dependent on the goodness of the receiver. This was the love God showed us through Christ Jesus.
[164] Ephesians 5:25

hates divorce."[165] This kept me wading through the attacks, and seeking to continue to love my wife like Christ loved the church. For it is written for us to, **"***Submit therefore to God. Resist the devil and he will flee from* [us]."[166] Finally, after many months of constant turmoil, **Christ gave me victory**! The cloud lifted, and because of standing on my Lord's Word, His grace, and the empowering of the Holy Spirit living within me, I had not crossed lines that would have devastated my marriage, but even more importantly, would have grieved my Lord. Beware brethren, when times of testing come your way, if you do not know God's Word, you will fail the test.[167] *"Be of sober spirit, be on the alert. Your adversary, the devil, prowls around like a roaring lion, seeking someone to devour."*[168]

God's Word on Divorce

Option One: The Unbelieving Spouse

"But to the rest I say, not the Lord, that if any brother has a wife who is an unbeliever, and she consents to live with him, he must not divorce her. And a woman who has an unbelieving husband, and he consents to live with her, she must not send her husband away...Yet if the unbelieving one leaves, let him leave; the brother or the sister is not under bondage in such cases, but God has called us to peace. For how do you know, O wife, whether you will save your husband? Or how do you know, O husband, whether you will save your wife?" [169]

---

[165] Malachi 2:16
[166] James 4:7
[167] James 1: 2, 13-15
[168] 1 Peter 5:8
[169] 1 Corinthians 7:12-14

If we examine the situation this passage speaks of, we see that it is not the option for the believer in Christ to divorce, but for the unbelieving spouse! If the spouse of the Christian, that is to say the one truly converted, chooses to leave, we see they are allowed to do so and the believer is to oblige. However, if they choose to stay, we are also to oblige in obedience to our Lord. This is what our Master would have of us, for we were bought with a price and are no longer our own, but His.

We walk a dangerous path when we skip over parts of God's Word to confirm our own desires. Therefore, let us again examine how we are called to treat our wives.

"Husbands, love your wives, just as Christ also loved the church and gave Himself up for her, so that He might sanctify her, having cleansed her by the washing of water with the word, that He might present to Himself the church in all her glory, having no spot or wrinkle or any such thing; but that she would be holy and blameless. So husbands ought also to love their own wives as their own bodies. He who loves his own wife loves himself; for no one ever hated his own flesh, but nourishes and cherishes it, just as Christ also does the church, because we are members of His body." [170]

We are commanded to love our wives as Christ loved the church, regardless of what they have done or will do to us. This love we are commanded, as born again Christian men, to follow in our every action with our wife. It is to love her sacrificially even when she least deserves it. The good news is that this love is given to us through the Holy Spirit as we submit to Christ, obeying His direction to us;

---

[170] Ephesians 5:25-30

certainly though, this is not based on our fickle feelings which are prone to fluctuate. This love is based instead on God's command, Christ's example, and on the commitment we made before God on our wedding day when we vowed to love her until death do us part. The above passage is one of the clearest New Testament passages regarding how we are to treat our wives; and I wholeheartedly believe that it leaves us no room for divorce.

Option Two: The Unfaithful Spouse

"It was said, 'WHOEVER SENDS HIS WIFE AWAY, LET HIM GIVE HER A CERTIFICATE OF DIVORCE'; but I say to you that everyone who divorces his wife, except for the reason of unchastity, makes her commit adultery; and whoever marries a divorced woman commits adultery." [171]

Let us consider the above passage in light of our command to *"love our wives like Christ loves the church."* Think for just a moment, how much does He love us? Our Savior sacrificially loved us even when we were least deserving of it. In spite of ourselves, He washed us, forgave us, and took our place. Oh, shall we not love our wives like He loved us – even if they sin against us? Yes! We are to forgive [172] them, washing them with the Word, thereby showing them Christ. However, if we choose not to forgive and send our wives away, causing them to remarry, not only do we fail to show forgiveness, but the one whom remarries her *"commits adultery."* Do I go too far in saying that we would have helped him into such sin and refused showing her grace?

---

[171] Matthew 5:31
[172] Matthew 6:15

In Matthew, where this subject is also found, we read, *"The disciples said to Him, 'If the relationship of the man with his wife is like this, it is better not to marry.' But He said to them, 'Not all men can accept this statement, but only those to whom it has been given.'"* [173] Dear brethren, God takes marriage seriously, very seriously, so seriously even the disciples thought it a costly thing to take a wife to themselves.

Oh Lord, keep our hearts soft and our conscience sensitive to the Holy Spirit. May we seek to follow You obediently, word by word.

What about Mercy?

> *"My little children, I am writing these things to you so that you may not sin. And if anyone sins, we have an Advocate with the Father, Jesus Christ the righteous; and He Himself is the propitiation for our sins; and not for ours only, but also for those of the whole world."* [174]

Let us for a moment consider our Lord's mercy regarding sin and marriage. Adultery is not an unpardonable sin, nor is divorce. [175] Christ's blood covers adultery and remarriage for even Christians; however, I believe there should be a Holy fear within us concerning our testing of the Lord in this matter. The sacred covenant broken with a spouse has lasting consequences, [176] but *"if we confess our sins, He is faithful and righteous to forgive us our sins and*

---

[173] Matthew 19:8-11
[174] 1 John 2:1-2
[175] Mark 3:28-30 reveals the only unpardonable sin
[176] Christ disqualifies those who do such from continuing in leadership positions in His church; not to mention the often lasting emotional and even spiritual scars

to cleanse us from all unrighteousness."[177] However as noted earlier, "*God can have mercy and forgive sin in remarriage even in Christian marriages. It* [however] *is not an example* [of Godly living, nor obedience to Christ,] *and even shameful to the church.*" "*What shall we say then? Are we to continue in sin so that grace may increase? May it never be! How shall we who died to sin still live in it?*"[178] We must remember that "*it is written,* 'YOU SHALL NOT PUT THE LORD YOUR GOD TO THE TEST.'"[179]

Conclusion

If we choose to listen to the world or many in the modern church, we are doomed to fail in our marriages. We can only rest on Christ and His clear Word if we desire that our marriages persevere. As we saw earlier, we can, through Christ, overcome even the greatest temptations if we will throw ourselves on His Holy Word. God is serious about marriage and has issued extreme measures within His commands to keep believing husbands one with their wives. While we can find forgiveness, there are still severe repercussions for transgressing the marriage covenant. In closing this chapter dear brethren, remember the Apostles Paul's command to us: "*Husbands, love your wives, just as Christ also loved the church.*" Let us make this of high importance and follow Christ, even to the death of ourselves. Let us serve as a witness to this fading world and even to our fellow brethren. But most importantly, let us serve to obey Him, who willingly gave His life for ours.

---

[177] 1 John 1:9
[178] Romans 6:23
[179] Matthew 4:6-7

From the Ladies

"It means he is following God's devine order – God is the head of Christ, Christ is the head of the husband, the husband is the head of the wife. It also means that following this way (God's way), loving Christ first will enable the man to love his wife all the more. I am not married, but I wouldn't like a husband who doesn't put Christ first. Our Father's ways are always best!

~ Blandine

Give Yourself Up

*F**or the husband is the head of the wife, as Christ also is the head of the church, He Himself being the Savior of the body.*[180] In the preceding text, there are two chief topics that deserve much heeding; it is to these I would like to briefly address. Because of these, a greater accountability on judgment day will be demanded of us husbands. Let us take heed and remember, if our wives are truly saved, she is a child of the Most High God. Her worth to Him is far greater than we can ever know, and something we must take far more seriously.

1. head –

Holding a position as *head* of the wife, *head* of the family, or even *head* in the church does not come with bragging rights. It does not come with management perks. It does not come with justifications for abuse. It does not come with a greater title. It *does* come with more accountability, responsibility, and if mistreated or misused, more

---

[180] Ephesians 5:23

weighted judgment from God. This position demands a relentless denial of self-pleasure, denial of self-gratification, and denial of self-promotion. It is a position that can send you straight to hell if willfully abused. Proper demonstration of this position is in the hidden hours spent in prayer behind closed doors. Outside of your immediate family, no one witnesses you in your headship/leadership for your wife and family. There is no glory to be attained. I have heard one preacher say, *"You start a church to care for the people of the church."*[181] To that I add, you marry a bride and even start a family to care for her and the children that were given to you in God's sovereignty.

A few years ago I was involved with youth ministry[182] as a leader at a small rural church. After about a year and a half my wife said something that convicted me greatly. I will never forget when she said, *"While you are out there saving the world, your wife and your children are at home dying."* She said it lovingly, she said it calm, and yet said it with power as a point of conviction was driven deep into my soul. The Spirit drove me to my knees and repentance was granted.

Husbands, love your wives and do not be embittered against them.[183]

When I became a husband my ministry, my service, and my work should have been birthed from within the context of home and that of closed doors ever before leaving into the public arena. I have to admit that I have not always

---

[181] Paul Washer
[182] very difficult if you are trying to be biblical because this is the father's job
[183] Colossians 3:19

been obedient in this area. When I had children, my work in the home has increasingly intensified. I must walk with my Lord starting in the home, and there as well be dedicated to my bride and lead my family into the truths of Christ. My wife and children are the first people to where my passion, my service, my life, and my work are to be directed. Does this mean I ignore the church and all its needs? No, but true ministry begins inside the home front. We are called to serve one another in the church and we are called to reach the lost, but we must remember there is perfect balance in Christ. We are never called to break one aspect of God's will in order to fulfill another aspect of His same will.[184]

I appeal to you therefore, brothers, by the mercies of God, to present your bodies as a living sacrifice, holy and acceptable to God, which is your spiritual worship.[185]

Apply the previous verse to your primary ministry – your marriage. I often hear many professing Christians who say they do not drink boasting in Ephesians 5:18, and yet they fall far short in following the next fourteen verses of Scripture. Having fewer problems in one area of life does not blanket the areas that are very much an area of complete failure. The Bible does not say you can't have a drink, it says don't be drunk; however the Bible gives no room to mistreat His daughter. How dare we make much of our victories in small things and make so little of our failures in big things, mainly our wives.

See to it that no one fails to obtain the grace of God; that no 'root of bitterness' springs up and causes trouble, and by it many become defiled.[186]

---

[184] Thought owed to Paul Washer
[185] Romans 12:1 - ESV

2. savior –

This brings us to our second topic, and it is this: *as Christ also is the head of the church, He Himself being the savior of the body.* This is mentioned so little, yet it carries with it such weight – *savior*.

It is not that our wives are saved through faith in us, nor can we produce any form of salvation, yet there is a strong sense in which we are to be the *savior as Christ* is of the church. For us to be like Christ we must set ourselves on a continual path in the declaration and demonstration of love, humility, and sanctification for our wives. The reality of our transformed heart, that work Christ has done in our lives, ought to be poured out onto and into our wives.

Therefore a man shall leave his father and his mother and hold fast to his wife, and they shall become one flesh.[187]

My wife is the only person that I am one flesh with. If this indeed is true and she is a part of my body, then how much more am I to be like Christ and give myself *up for her?*[188] We are to nourish our bride. We *are not* called to die for *His* bride and then sacrifice our wife and families in the name of ministry; Christ has done this! We *are* called to be *as Christ* and die for *our* bride, and when we do so we become like Christ – savior to our wives.

Regarding these two topics, *head of the wife* and *savior of the body*, we husbands must take heed and stay alert in our

---

[186] Hebrews 12:14-15
[187] Genesis 2:24
[188] Ephesians5:25

position. We must not abuse our *headship* role and we must live a life of authenticity in our *savior* role. The power to effectively carry out our duty is birthed through the grace of God and grows to mature more and more through sanctification. God honoring actions in our privileged position as a husband is founded in the authentic reality of the new birth being rooted in Christ Himself. Being made aware of our position, this through the Scriptures, increases our responsibility, and demands our conformity to act and make decisions in a God-honor style of life. Knowledge of what we ought to do, without repentance, is not wisdom, and thus leads us down a damning dark path of disobedience as we neglect our leadership. I wonder, what does our leadership and love look like, right now, through the eyes of our wives? Maybe we should sit down and actually ask them. Is it not time to give ourselves up for the purposes of Christ, to be *as Christ*?

And He Himself bore our sins in His body on the cross, so that we might die to sin and live to righteousness; for by His wounds you were healed.[189]

You husbands in the same way, live with your wives in an understanding way, as with someone weaker, since she is a woman; and show her honor as a fellow heir of the grace of life, so that your prayers will not be hindered.[190]

---

[189] 1 Peter 2:24
[190] 1 Peter 3:7

From the Ladies

Eve was created for Adam by God removing a rib from Adam's body and creating it into the woman that would become he wife and help mate, the two become one. The husband is to love his wife as Christ loves his bride the church. The woman is to honor her husband. One truly born again, filled with the Holy Spirit, has the love of God within their heart and is a brand new creature in Christ. This is why it is so important for the husband to be born again – he is to be head over his household. The wife also must be born again, the two equally yoked together, both serving the Lord together, training their children up in the ways of the Lord; this was, and still is, God's ultimate plan in marriage. This means everything to me and I desire my husband to always be a follower of Jesus Christ, a strong leader, a light in our family, filled with the love of God – God first and family second. Wives we must pray daily for our husbands.

~ Lynn

Final Thoughts
Welcome to Manhood

We have been sent on a great commission indeed; launched forward to *make disciples of all the nations, baptizing them in the name of the Father and the Son and the Holy Spirit, teaching them to observe all that was commanded.*[191] We are to *go into all the world and preach the gospel.*[192] We are to proclaim repentance and forgiveness of sins.[193] And yet, if you are a husband, you have before you a ministry, an opportunity to engage eternity, and a mission in this darkened day like no other. Regardless of the times and the culture in which we live, if we are a husband, then our marching orders are clear cut.

You may be thinking, *"Why is he saying this at the end?"* The commissioning of Christ is to every regenerated soul and we need to reach every person in the world with the gospel by being *salt and light.* We must be indigenous missionaries right where we live, but if indeed you are

---

[191] Matthew 28:19-20
[192] Mark 16:15
[193] Luke 24:47

married, then how do you think you can carry out the great commission if you are outside the will of God in your home? Any ministry you are involved with better begin in depths of Christ, behind the doors of your home, in service to your wife, and if in God's providence you have children, in their training and upbringing. If God wills for you to fulfill a specific task, He will always work it in such a way that He will never contradict Himself.

Having said this, let us be reminded, we need to take our walk with God and our positions as husbands deadly serious. We must remember that *"whoever knows the right thing to do and fails to do it, for him it is sin."*[194] This takes the application of the Scriptures to a very deep and personal level, one between God and us alone. What shall we do? Shall we say we are men of God, Christians, and then not do the *good* that we *know* we *ought*? Lord give us the strength and wisdom to act accordingly.

So, what areas are you in need of repentance? Are you seeking the Father's presence for yourself and for your family? Are you biblically loving your wife in and through the reality of regeneration? Are you accepting the full responsibility of loving and teaching your children?

These words, which I am commanding you today, shall be on your heart. You shall teach them diligently to your sons and shall talk of them when you sit in your house and when you walk by the way and when you lie down and when you rise up. You shall bind them as sign on your head and they shall be as frontals on your forehead. You shall write them on the doorposts of your house and on your gates.[195]

---

[194] James 4:17
[195] Deuteronomy 6:6-9

You might be thinking, *"This is a lot of hard work,"* well, you are correct. Let me just say it, this is the point – be a man. *"God is not raising boy scouts, He's raising up soldiers."[196]*

"Welcome to manhood. You go to bed every night tired. You come home from work only to realize your work has just begun. The fact that you are the provider for your family means absolutely nothing; that is just one tiny aspect of a greater commission."[197]

Knowledge of repentance, without obedience to the Spirit, is not repentance. Knowledge of God's wrath, yet without a heeding of His Word, is not fear of the Lord. Claiming to be a Christian, without visible fruits of conversion, does not provide evidence you are a Christian. Make sure your salvation is a reality and not a deception. Make sure your sanctification is a true work of God and not some emotional lie. Make certain your calling and election.[198]

Welcome to manhood.

---

[196] Leonard Ravenhill
[197] Paul Washer – message, *The Christian Husband* – sermonaudio.com
[198] 2 Peter 1:10

From the Ladies

"As we talked, our journeys are different. And while my husband believes in God and is seeking His will for his life, he has many past issues he has not yet chosen to give to God. My desire for my husband is to put God first in all things. The Word places the husband as 'head of the house' and if my husband is struggling to live according to God's will, then there is tension. I understand it is our responsibility to work out our own salvation, as my husband's walk is between him and God. If my husband puts God first in all things, then he would understand the 'peace that surpasses all understanding'. Recently, I was diagnosed with breast cancer. I find rest and peace with my Father and I am not concerned with the ultimate outcome; as I know the journey is for the good and it will bring Glory to God's Kingdom. The enemy has been very successful with reminding my husband what poor choices he has made in the past and my husband struggles to move beyond the past. I want my husband to be free from the past, free from the enemy's ability to stir up guilt and shame, so that he might live victorious in Christ Jesus. If my husband put God first in all things, the enemy would have to go away and my husband would be free."

~ Wenda

We urge you, brethren, admonish the unruly, encourage the fainthearted, help the weak, be patient with everyone. See that no one repays another with evil for evil, but always seek after that which is good for one another and for all people. Rejoice always; pray without ceasing; in everything give thanks; for this is God's will for you in Christ Jesus. Do not quench the Spirit; but examine everything carefully; hold fast to that which is good; abstain from every form of evil.[199]

---

[199] 1 Thessalonians 5:14-22

As Christ ~ A Man and Marriage

Brief Ponderings
from George Whitefield
Excerpts from his sermon, "*The Great Duty of Family Religion*"

Ponderings # 1

"And this will appear, if we consider that every governor of a family ought to look upon himself as obliged to act in three capacities: as a prophet, to instruct; as a priest, to pray for and with; as a king, to govern, direct, and provide for them.

"It is true indeed, the latter of these, their kingly office, they are not so frequently deficient in (what's more, in this they are generally too solicitous), but as for the two former, their priestly and prophetic offices, like Gallio, they care for no such things. But however indifferent some governors may be about it, they may be assured that God will require a due discharge of these offices at their hands. For if, as the apostle argues, '*He that does not provide for his own house,*'[200] in temporal things, '*has denied the faith, and is worse than an infidel,*' to what greater degree of apostasy must he have arrived who takes no thought to provide for the spiritual welfare of his family?"

---

[200] 1 Timothy 5:8

Ponderings #2

"Was a minister to disregard teaching his people publicly, and from house to house, and to excuse himself by saying that he had enough to do to work out his own salvation with fear and trembling, without concerning himself with that of others; would you not be apt to think such a minister to be like the unjust judge, 'one that neither feared God, nor regarded man?' And yet, odious as such a character would be, it is no worse than that governor of a family deserves, who thinks himself obliged only to have his own soul, without paying any regard to the souls of his household."

Ponderings #3

"It is true indeed, parents seldom forget to provide for their children's bodies (though, it is to be feared, some men are so far sunk beneath the beasts that perish, as to neglect even that), but then how often do they forget, or, rather, when do they remember, to secure the salvation of their immortal souls? But is this their way of expressing their fondness for the fruit of their bodies? Is this the best testimony they can give of their affections to the darling of their hearts? Then was Delilah found of Samson, when she delivered him up into the hands of the Philistines? Then were those ruffians well affected to Daniel, when they threw him into a den of lions?"

Ponderings #4

"Some motives to consider in order to excite all governors, with their respective households, to serve the Lord...

1. "The first motive I shall mention is *the duty of gratitude*, which you that are governors of families owe to God."

2. "But second, if gratitude to God will not, I think *love and pity to your children* should move you, with your respective families, to serve the Lord."

3. "But third, if neither gratitude to God nor love and pity to your children will prevail on you, yet let a *principle of common honesty and justice* move you to set up the holy resolution in the text."

4. "But fourth, if neither gratitude to God, pity to children, nor a principle for common justice to servants are sufficient to balance all objections; yet let that darling, that prevailing, *motive of self-interest* turn the scale and engage you with your respective households to serve the Lord."

5. "Fifth and last, if neither gratitude to God, love to your children, common justice to your servants, nor even that most prevailing motive self-interest, will excite; yet *let a consideration of the terrors of the Lord persuade you* to put in practice the pious resolution in the text.

"Remember, the time will come, and that perhaps very shortly, when we must all appear before the judgment seat of Christ; where we must give a solemn and strict account how we have had our conversation, in our respective families in this world. How will you endure to see your children and servants (who ought to be your joy and crown of rejoicing in the day of our Lord Jesus Christ) coming out as so many swift witnesses against you; cursing the father that begot them, the womb that bore them, the paps which they have sucked, and the day they ever entered into your houses? Think you not, the damnation which men must endure for their own sins will be sufficient that they need load themselves with the additional guilt of being accessory to the damnation of others also? Oh, consider this, all you that forget to serve the Lord with your respective households, 'lest he pluck you away, and there be none to deliver you'!"

From the Ladies

"It means my husband is the representation of Christ to me. He ministers to my needs and the needs of our family, just as Jesus loves His bride. My husband's words are to be received with humility and joy. This doesn't take me off the hook from drawing near to Christ myself; rather, it encourages and deepens my walk with Jesus, thus enables me to be a greater influence on my family and community. In this way, my husband is given the freedom to be all who Christ created him to be.

Following the voice of Jesus into his purpose and calling brings my husband into the joy of living the abundant life – even if we must walk the path of poverty or persecution.

My husband is not Christ and hence imperfect, so there are a checks and balances which need to be humbly put in place. When I see him stumble in his weakness, I can prayerfully lift him up, although sometimes this can be messy."

~ Libby

A Story: One Man's Journey

I was married at 22 without really having any idea of what it meant to be a Biblical husband. Unfortunately, I received very little advice on what I should expect as a husband or how I should be expected to live with my wife. My view of marriage was that I would continue living for myself and doing all the things I had always done but I would now have a beautiful woman to be with me and fulfill all my selfish needs and desires.

For much of my married life, I had the attitude that it was my job to go to work and then come home and do whatever I liked. I loved watching sports, playing sports, hanging out with friends or family, as well as a number of other activities. However, I believed that it was my wife's job to clean the house, pay the bills, raise the kids, as well as to provide for all of my selfish needs. I also blamed her for anything and everything that was wrong or didn't go the way I wanted it to. Whether it was a mess that one of the kids made or an error in the checkbook I pretty much put the blame on her and made sure that she knew it was her fault.

One of the worst parts of all for my wife wasn't the work that I expected of her, but the years I neglected to verbally affirm my love for her. I criticized her for everything imaginable but couldn't bring myself to ever give her a kind word. I couldn't even tell her that she was beautiful and that I loved her. She was so starved for that kind of affirmation but I was unable to see or understand. It was only the grace of God that sustained us both.

Truly the grace of God made the difference in our marriage. Although I wasn't doing very well in marriage, the Lord had been working on me for years and bringing me to the place that I needed to be. Through different people and circumstances the Lord showed me how I much I had failed as a husband and father. I began to pray that the Lord would change me and forgive me for everything that I had been involved with. While I'm not sure exactly how long I prayed for this, the Lord in His mercy began to change me and gave me the understanding of what it meant to love my wife as Christ loved the church.

At this point neither my wife nor I would say we are where we want to be in many areas of our life or marriage however we know that God is working in us to fulfill his purpose. I still struggle to give the kind word and restrain myself from being critical or angry; I know that this is sin and that I am still in need of His grace. I continue to struggle, repent and grow and above all trust in the righteousness of Christ as my very own.

"I have been crucified with Christ. It is no longer I who live, but Christ who lives in me. And the life I now live in the flesh I live by faith in the Son of God, who loved me and gave himself for me." - Galatians 2:20

~ Michael Melton[201]

---

[201] Close friend and brother in Christ

From the Ladies

"It is an honor to be married to a man who follows Christ. I also believe that it is the Lord's grace operating in my life, that I am married to a man who desires to know and serve Him. I have known my husband for almost 20 years and I have witnessed how Christ has changed him. Through his conforming to Christ, I have a greater understanding of walking in truth. My husband has been my teacher, my confidant, and my shelter. He loves sacrificially, prays for me and desires to see us grow in Christ. I also believe that God is glorified through a marriage that has been surrendered to Him. Though I may never fully comprehend what it means for my husband to be Christ-like in his love toward me, I know that I have experienced it in our marriage."

~ Stacy

For if anyone thinks that he is something when he is nothing, he deceives himself.[202]

---

[202] Galatians 6:3

From the Ladies

"To have my husband lead our family in Christ often puts me on my knees praising the Lord! It confirms that God is real, for flesh alone can't lead in love like this without the Holy Spirit. I know and experience my Lord and Savior through my husband; for I know and see Christ operating in my life through my husband. His best love is none other than the love of Christ through him. I feel the love not only from my husband but the inexpressible graciousness of Christ. It is one of peace, understanding and holiness. It is all encompassing, healthy and selfless. I often surrender to it and want to submit and give myself to its Originator. This doesn't mean that for me there isn't sometimes an internal fight or a process of sanctification but rather I cry out in prayer for God to walk with me; and He does. The thought of so many women needing and wanting this kind of leadership born out of God's perfect love, and not receiving it, burdens me, as I'm sure it burdens the Lord. If men could stop running and doing to please the Lord, or themselves, and love their wives as God has so clearly asked them, He would be far well pleased. Children's lives would forever be changed to see this love in action.

I experience God on a daily basis knowing that the blessings He bestows on us are not selflessly consumed by my husband alone. My Lord looks to my best interest for the Kingdom ahead. Most days I praise the Lord for what He has given me according to my needs and this also includes what He has not given me. I thank Him for giving me much, yet not all I think I need. He knows me better than I know myself and this includes the gift of my husband in all he is or he isn't. I thank God for growing my husband into the man He wills him to be, and that includes for leading me and my children. My husband is not perfect but I know the Lord is his Savior and He is in his greatest hope – completely submitted to him. I can do nothing but praise the Lord because I know He is in our home and I thank Him that our home is a sanctuary for Jesus. Victory in Christ! My prayer continues for the woman of this world to yet see this come to fruition for themselves. It makes every difference now and in my eternal future that my husband is a man seeking hard after the Lord Jesus Christ!"

~ Trish

From the Ladies

"It means he becomes Christ-like, and ultimately if we wives follow him, we try to become Christ-like too."

~ Paula

.

With everyday that I grow in sanctification, I realize how much more sin is yet still in me and how much more desperately I need God's grace, conviction, repentance, joy, peace, patience, and power in my life, especially in regards to my marriage. If you have been searching the Bible for an *out clause* in your marriage, there is not one. Any fleshly justification to void the marriage that you have agreed to is sin and needs immediate repentance.

~ Author ~

From the Ladies

"My husband is confident as a lion... tender hearted as a lamb. I am blessed when we are in agreement. I trust the Lord to 'download' His truths and His will when we aren't in agreement. He may not always listen to me, but he wants to hear from the Lord. He turns to Christ for guidance and strength. He is Christ-like by his sacrificial lifestyle. He sanctifies my life, by the washing of the Word. My husband's life is a part of my destiny in Christ."

~ Elizabeth

For God has not called us for the purpose of impurity, but in sanctification.[203]

"We are ambassadors of the Lord Jesus Christ with everything we do and say."[204]

---

[203] 1 Thessalonians 4:7
[204] Warren Judge

bio

Jeremy B. Strang
Christian, husband, father of five and author.

Other books:

The Foothills of True Grace
Realities of a True Christian
Reveling or Resisting
Christian ~ A Dangerous Title To Claim
Limiting God?

www.jeremybstrang.com

In the spirit of George Whitefield, *"May the name of Jeremy Strang turn to dust and forever disappear so long as the name of Jesus Christ is exalted."*

A book is to be written and used in such a way that it brings glory to God, draws us closer to God's actual presence, and leads us into His Word. If these foundational and essential rules are not evident, nor a true reality, then the book was conceived of the flesh, written apart from the Spirit, and read in vain; thus directing the reader away from God and increasing judgment upon the author.

Made in the USA
San Bernardino, CA
28 June 2017